ONE CONNECTION

How You Can Grow Your Business (and Change the World) One Connection at a Time

Kevin Willett

Kevin Willett

One Connection: How You Can Grow Your Business (and Change the World) One Connection at a Time
Copyright © 2015 by Kevin Willett
All Rights Reserved

ISBN-13: 978-1512034028

ISBN-10: 1512034029

One Connection

TABLE OF CONTENTS

TABLE OF CONTENTS 3
INTRODUCTION 5
ETIQUETTE 9
PHILOSOPHY 23
TIME MANAGEMENT 43
BEFORE EVENTS 51
DURING EVENTS 61
AFTER EVENTS 79
BUSINESS CARDS 83
SOCIAL MEDIA 87
AFTERWORD 95

Kevin Willett

INTRODUCTION

I'd like to tell you about my first networking event. I have to admit, I was scared and didn't know what to expect. I showed up, filled in my name badge, turned around, and realized I didn't know anyone in the room. So I started to panic a little and felt like I was back at the old CYO dances. Who should I talk to? What should I say? Luckily for me, an older gentleman came up to me and said, "Son, you have a deer-in-the-headlights look. I take it this is your first networking event?" I smiled and said, "Yes." He spent some time talking with me and introduced me to a few people. After I spoke with three people, I'd reached my goal, so I ripped off my name badge and left to pick up a pizza and a Mountain Dew and go home and relax, proud of myself that I made it through.

Since then, I've started two networking groups. I host 20 monthly networking events, a radio show, and a video show, and I've built a social media following of over 20,000 people.

If I was able to go from that nervous guy at his first networking event to someone who makes his living hosting those events, rest assured that you can become a successful networker, building relationships that help your business thrive, one connection at a time.

"I don't know how to network."

I hear that a lot from people who attend my events. Little did I realize that those seven words would be the biggest challenge I'd face when I started the Friends of

Kevin Willett

Kevin networking group. I'm not sure why I'm still surprised when I hear them, but I am.

Networking is the most affordable way to grow your business. We like to do business with people we know, like, and trust. Think about the last time you were looking for a contractor or a mechanic or a hair salon or just about anything. I'll bet you asked your friends who they would recommend. I understand that attending networking events is uncomfortable for most people. But it's an essential tool to grow your business.

The first time you get out there it may not be easy. You may be thinking:

"Oh my God, I'm scared."

"I hope I don't say anything stupid."

"Where do I put this silly name badge?"

"How long do I have to stay here?"

"Who should I talk to?"

"I hope people like me."

"Is it okay to eat and drink?"

"What am I supposed to do with all of these business cards?"

"This is awkward. I'm standing all by myself."

I'm sure you get the picture. My friends, it's only natural to have thoughts like these because most people are not comfortable walking into a room full of people they've never met. It will get better!

This book offers tips on what to do before, during, and after a networking event. These tips are a guide to help you feel comfortable and be successful at presenting yourself and your business. Both experienced and new networkers will benefit from reading this book. If you have any questions about any of the tips or you need advice on business networking, email me at Kevin@friendsofkevin.com. I love talking about networking! I'm always interested in seeing the challenges of networking through the eyes of other people. That makes me a better networker, so thanks for helping me out. I hope to see you at one of my networking events.

Kevin Willett

ETIQUETTE

THE GOLDEN RULE OF NETWORKING: HELP OTHERS BEFORE YOU HELP YOURSELF

We all know that networking is about building trust and getting people to know, like, and trust us. But sometimes we forget. We get excited and go right into our sales pitch. You should buy my widgets. (I use the word widgets so that I don't offend anyone. If you sell widgets don't worry. I'm not talking about you.) Of course, when no one buys our widgets, we get mad and stop networking because it's stupid and doesn't work.

Let me suggest a different approach. Next time you attend a networking event, focus on helping the people you're speaking with. Ask them a few questions about their businesses. Find out who would be good clients for them. Try to think of people you know who may be good referral sources for them and ask if they'd like to meet those people. Typically, people will be so excited that you offered to help them, without trying to sell them anything, that they'll ask how they can help you. Notice that you didn't have to ask for help. They volunteered.

You might be thinking, "But Kevin, what if they don't offer to help you back?" That's okay, just consider it a deposit in the karma bank. Never keep score or expect a referral from everyone you give a referral to. Life doesn't work that way. Always do the right thing for the right reason and things will work out for you.

THE IMPORTANCE OF MAKING DEPOSITS IN THE KARMA BANK

Whenever people ask me to help them, I ask myself one question: "Is this the right thing to do?" Don't always focus on whether or not you can make money from helping a friend. Doing that will give you wicked bad karma.

Let me tell you a story. Recently a friend asked me to help out a mutual friend who was starting a professional soccer club. I could have said, "Hey, I'd love to help but he needs to pay to be a client." Instead, I asked myself whether this was the right thing to do. My answer was yes, because this friend rarely asks for favors from me and I think it's super cool that our friend has the courage to start a professional soccer club. So I started sharing his updates on Facebook to help him raise awareness of the club.

Fast forward six months. Someone connected with me on social media who was perfect for Friends of Kevin, one of my networking groups. You probably guessed the ending. Turns out he's friends with the guys from the soccer club. Because I'd made those deposits in the karma bank, I was able to ask them to put in a good word for me and I picked up a new client. Please understand, you shouldn't expect good things to happen because you helped a friend. But they usually do.

YODA WAS CORRECT

The great Yoda said there is do or do not but there is no try. Kevin says there is yes or no but there is no maybe.

Many business owners spend a lot of time preparing quotes for clients, only to never hear back from them. My friends, if someone takes the time to quote a job for you, please show them the respect of giving an answer, even if it's no. I often have great ideas to grow my business. Sadly, many of them are outside my budget. It can be awkward to tell business owners that I can't afford their services or products, but I tell them. Let's think about this. What if someone who prepared a quote for you came across a really great potential client for you? Do you really think he or she would refer you if you never bothered to respond to the quote? Probably not, because he or she may believe you'll show the same disrespect to the client. Remember, my friends, it all comes down to respect.

DO WHAT YOU SAY YOU'LL DO

Last week two people sent me emails asking for help. I responded, "Sure, give me a call tomorrow and I can help you." Both said they'd call me the next day. It's been a few weeks and I haven't heard from either of them. I know things come up, but think about the message they're sending. They're being disrespectful and more importantly they're showing that they're unreliable. My friends, nobody wants to do business with unreliable people. If you tell someone you're going to do something and you forget, call and apologize, but please don't tell them how busy you are. Do you know anyone who isn't busy? Most people will understand and give you a second chance.

RETURN CALLS AND EMAILS

I have to admit, as my business has grown, I've struggled with time management and returning calls and emails. My friends, there's no excuse for it, so I'm sorry if I've let any of you down. We're all busy, but if something's important to us, we'll make the time to get it done. The message you send by not returning emails or phone calls is that the person reaching out to you isn't important. Is that the message you want to send? You don't need to stay up all night going through emails and voicemails. But a quick response within 24 hours is a proper courtesy, even if you just let them know you got the message and will get back to them with a full response soon.

STAY IN CONTACT

Do you have friends who only call you when they need something? That doesn't make you feel special, right? Yet many of us treat our business contacts that way. I have a few friends who only call me when they need something. Now, I'm a professional connector so it's part of my job, but I encourage you to reach out to your contacts on a regular basis, even if it's just to say hi and see if you can help them with anything. How often should you reach out to them? It depends upon the relationship you have or want with the contact. If someone is a great client or referral source for you, I'd recommend you contact them monthly or every other month. Otherwise quarterly is fine. Just be sure to actually contact them on a consistent basis. I guarantee you'll be amazed by the results.

THE POWER OF SAYING THANK YOU

I was having a soda with a friend who was upset. He had worked hard to find a great referral for a friend who never called to thank him. In fact, he was so upset that I don't think he'll refer that friend again. I have to be honest, I was leaning back in the chair thinking about all the times I forgot to say thank you. So stop reading this book for a minute and call or email a friend to thank him or her for trying to help you. It doesn't matter if the referral worked out or not. Call and say, "Hey, I appreciate you trying to help me." You might be surprised by the positive impact it has on your business.

SOMEBODY'S ALWAYS WATCHING

I had an issue a few weeks ago with the local coffee shop. I went in to pick up the coffee I'd ordered the day before. The young woman behind the counter screamed at me, "Well did you pre-order it? You can't just walk in and expect it to be ready." I have to admit, I really wanted to scream back at her, but I looked over my shoulder to see all these people looking at me. If I gave in to the temptation to scream back, they would have said, "Geez, look at Kevin. He thinks he's so important that he's yelling at the poor girl." So I smiled and said, "Yes I did, yesterday afternoon. I'm sure someone forgot to leave a note for you. Can you make one up for me?" Understand that you are your brand and everything you say and do is a reflection of you and your company.

I FORGOT YOUR NAME

I'm really good at remembering the names of people who attend my networking events. Sometimes, if I see you in public, that may be a little harder. Now, don't be insulted. It's just that we all look different outside of "business mode." You weren't wearing sweatpants and a ball cap at the event, and oh, you were wearing contacts, not glasses. If you see me at the store and I have that "Oh my, I don't remember your name" look, please say, "Hello, Kevin. It's me, John." I would really appreciate that.

So what do you do if this happens to you? You have two strategies. The first and best way is to say you're sorry, but his name is escaping you. Option two, which I admit I use from time to time, is to grab the person you're with and say something like, "Hello, have you met my friend John?" Often the person will say, "Hello John, I'm Kevin." It works and saves you the embarrassment of having to admit you forgot the person's name.

DON'T RANDOMLY ADD PEOPLE TO YOUR NEWSLETTER LIST

Have you ever given someone your business card at a networking event and found yourself on his or her newsletter list? It's happened to all of us. Let me be clear, just because I give you my card or you find it at the local pizza house, it doesn't mean I'm giving you permission to add me to your newsletter list. *Always* ask for permission or email a link to sign up for your newsletter. Otherwise, you're sending spam, which is illegal and could get your email marketing account closed (in which case, you'll probably lose your list). When I receive unsolicited newsletters, I email the sender asking him or her to refresh my memory as to where we met. I understand that we're all trying to grow our lists because our marketing people tell us how important it is. But if nobody's reading your newsletter, is it really helping you grow your business?

BLUETOOTH

I like to say, unless you're protecting the president of the United States, please remove your Bluetooth. It doesn't make you look cool, it makes you look unapproachable. Many years ago, I was involved in a networking group. One young guy would come to the events with this flashing blue light in his ear. This was before anyone had a Bluetooth, so everyone assumed he must have a really important job. More importantly, nobody would talk to him because we didn't know what he did and we didn't know if he was listening to someone. Eventually he told the group leader he wasn't getting any referrals from the group and nobody was even talking to him. I asked the leader if he wanted me to fix this problem. So I walked over to the guy, pulled his Bluetooth out, placed it in his shirt pocket, and told him, "You're not protecting the president of the United States, so take out your Bluetooth if you want people to talk to you." You may have already guessed that this guy worked at the cell phone store.

I MESSED UP TODAY

I'm embarrassed to admit that, for the first time in six years, I forgot an appointment. I have to be honest, when the guy called me, I was tempted to lie and say we were scheduled for 11 a.m., not 10 a.m., or that I had it in my calendar for the following week. Luckily, I caught myself. Why should I lie to him? He knows I messed up. Lying to him will only make it worse. My friends, we all make mistakes, so when you do, admit it and tell the person you're sorry. Most people will forgive you, and if they don't, that's okay too. Either way, reschedule and move on, but do it honestly.

GIVE PEOPLE THE BENEFIT OF THE DOUBT

I received a call from a potential client asking questions about my networking group. Honestly, she was asking them in an almost defensive way. I was in the middle of something, so I could hear myself being short with her. Luckily, I caught myself, took a deep breath, and slowly and clearly answered her questions. Throughout this book you'll hear me say, "Is that the image you want to project?" Think about this. I came really close to telling her the group wasn't for her and hanging up on her. What type of image is that? A really bad one, my friends. If my name came up in conversation, she might say "I called him and he told me the group wasn't for me and hung up on me." So be patient, always do your best to answer questions, and give people the benefit of the doubt.

DON'T SPEAK BADLY ABOUT PEOPLE

You may be thinking this is common sense. But I always say if it were common, everyone would know it. Back in my corporate days, I met a printer at a networking event. He asked me who we used for our printing. When I told him, he said, "That guy isn't in jail yet?" I became concerned and asked him why my printer should be in jail. After speaking with him for a few minutes, it became obvious that he didn't like my printer because he had much lower prices and was picking up a lot of his clients. After that statement, do you think I'd ever do business with him? Of course not. The only comment you should ever make is something along the lines of "It's a great company that does a great job." Bad mouthing your competition is a horrible idea. Focus your energy on providing the best customer experience possible for your clients and not on cutting down the reputation of the competition.

I WAS ONLY 45 MINUTES LATE. WHAT'S THE BIG DEAL?

Last week I planned on meeting a new business owner at 10 a.m. 10:15 came along and he still wasn't there, so I called and emailed him. By 10:30 there was still no response, so I figured something came up and I left. At 10:45 he called to ask where I was. I explained to him that we were supposed to meet at 10 a.m., so at 10:30 I gave up and left, which seemed to upset him. He said, "I told you I was coming. Why didn't you keep waiting? I was doing some other stuff, but it's no big deal. We were just meeting for coffee and it's not like the meeting was important or you're a client or anything." I have to admit, for once I was actually speechless. I tried to explain to him that it was disrespectful to leave me sitting there, that he should have returned my call or email, but I knew he just didn't get it. So show of hands, how many people think he'll be in business three months from now? I have a few friends who are perpetually late by at least 15 minutes and I'm sorry, my friends, there are no excuses for this. The solution is simple: Leave 15 minutes earlier. If you're constantly late, you're sending the message that your time is more valuable than mine. I can't trust you to show up on time if I refer you. Is that the message you want to send?

DON'T ASK ME OUT

When I first started speaking about business networking, I asked my friends to share some of their tips with me. A female friend said, "Can you remind guys that just because I'm single, doesn't mean it's okay to ask me out on a date?" I was surprised. She told me someone had asked her if she wanted to "network" with him on Saturday night at 8 p.m. at a fancy Italian restaurant. I think we can all agree that the guy is clearly asking her for a date. Be careful about crossing that line at a business event. Not only is it the wrong place and wrong time, but you look like a creeper. I don't think you want that reputation. Networking and dating have a lot of similarities. We put on our best outfit and use our most charming personality, hoping everyone will like us. But just because the cute guy or girl smiled at you doesn't mean he or she wants to date you.

PHONE ETIQUETTE – ALWAYS BE NICE TO PEOPLE

A potential client emailed me asking me for more information about my networking groups. I phoned him, because it's much easier to describe the groups and answer questions about them by phone rather than exchanging many emails. When I called, he said he was busy and asked me to call back in a few days. When I called back and said, "Hello, this is Kevin calling," he replied, "I know who you are and I don't have time to speak with you" and hung up. I have to admit, I was shocked. We've all had times when we handled a situation badly. I know that I've wanted my share of "do-overs." But when you mishandle a situation like that, pick up the phone and apologize. Most people will forgive you. Because he didn't apologize, I'd never even consider having him as a client and I of course could never refer him, because he might treat my clients the way he treated me. So next time you're tempted to be short with someone on the phone, ask yourself if that's the image you want that person to have of you.

HOW NOT TO ASK SOMEONE TO LUNCH

A woman I hardly knew emailed me asking if I'd meet her for lunch. I suspect most people would have deleted the email. Luckily, I'm not most people, so I replied to her message, asking why she wanted to meet. She responded with a legitimate reason, so I agreed to the meeting. If you're asking people you don't know well to go to lunch, *please* explain why you want to meet them. And please don't use the line "I'd just like to pick your brain." (See the next tip for more on that.) One more very important point: Don't lie. A woman asked to meet me to learn more about my networking group, saying she might like to join. When I arrived, she told me she lied to get me there, because she knew that once I saw her network marketing 30-minute video, I'd want to join her company and invite all my friends and she would make a lot of money. Okay, for those of you playing at home, how many people think I joined the company? Of course I didn't. I explained to her that she really shouldn't lie. And oh, by the way, she had no intention of joining the group. How can I possibly invite her to events or find her referrals when she's dishonest? So never lie to get people to meet you. Ninety-nine percent of the time it's going to end badly and your reputation will suffer.

CAN I PICK YOUR BRAIN?

This is probably the worst question you can ask someone. Many of my friends struggle with how to answer it. If you truly have a quick question, it's probably acceptable to ask it. If you hope to walk away with your marketing plan for next year, you totally crossed the line. If you do ask to meet with someone to pick their brain, make it convenient for them. Someone in Concord, NH, asked to pick my brain and said he was busy, so it would be best for him if I could drive up to Concord. So you want me to drive roughly 45 minutes both ways so you can pick my brain for free? I'm sure you can see why that's not acceptable. Also, when you meet with someone, purchase his or her beverage or meal. Never allow him or her to pay for anything. You're asking for free help, so the meeting shouldn't cost the person a dime.

Kevin Willett

PHILOSOPHY

BE CONSISTENT

My friends, networking is not something you only do when you need new clients. You must be consistent about attending events. I have a few friends who network like crazy when their sales pipeline is dry, then stop networking so they can meet up with all the people they met at the events. And then they start the cycle all over again by networking like crazy to meet more people. I think it makes much more sense to attend one or two events a week to keep people in your sales pipeline, rather than trying to attend five events in one week and then not show up anywhere for another month. You never want to disappear and make people wonder where you are.

THE SECRET TO BEING SUCCESSFUL WITH BUSINESS NETWORKING

I'm going to give you the key to being successful with business networking. Are you ready? I read a book a few weeks ago that said if you want to be successful, study the people in your industry who are successful and simply do what they do. That made me think about business networking. Are there traits all successful networkers have? I think the trait they have in common is that they participate in the groups they're involved in. They take a leadership role in the group, they help the new members in the group be successful, and they make time to meet with people outside of the regular meetings/events to build relationships. So the key to being successful with business networking is to fully participate.

BE FIRST

When I was a little boy, I used to go to boxing matches. I'd always hear the expression "Be first," which means punch first. I just realized that this applies to networking also. People often tell me they're in a referral-based networking group, but they don't receive referrals from certain members of the group. My first question is, "Have you ever passed them a referral?" Typically, the answer is, "No, I haven't met anyone who needs their services." I always encourage them to do three things.

First, search hard for a referral for them or introduce them to someone who may be a great referral partner (referral partners are people who can consistently pass references to each other, like a realtor and a mortgage broker).

Second, do coffee meetings with those people to educate them about your business and help them find referrals for you. One common answer I get is, "But Kevin, I'm a realtor. Everyone knows what I do." Not true, my friends. Most of my realtor friends have niches they specialize in. There's something unique about every business owner, so take the time to meet with those members and educate them about what's unique about you.

Third, don't be shy about asking for referrals. If you have clients who are happy with your work, ask them to introduce you to their friends who may need your services. I can often be shy about asking for referrals. But think about it. If I meet you, of course I'm going to tell you my networking group is great. What am I supposed to tell you, that it stinks? It's so much more powerful when members of my group tell you that it's great. Eighty-five percent of my clients come from referrals from existing clients. Now do you understand why you should ask your clients for referrals?

DON'T CRY OVER SPILLED MILK

I was reading about national Don't Cry Over Spilled Milk Day and that got me thinking about networking. It's funny how everything makes me think about networking. A few deals I was working on fell apart unexpectedly, and I have to admit, it deflated me. But as business owners, we can't concentrate on the deals that didn't happen. We have to focus on the next deal. So at the end of each day, focus on two or three things that went well and not on the things that didn't.

QUALITY OVER QUANTITY

I went to a networking event recently and only eight people attended. I was disappointed, because I had lots to do that day. But I remembered that I'm always telling people it's quality over quantity when it comes to connections. Of those eight people, two were really great contacts for me. Let's be honest, most of us have skipped a networking event because we saw that the event registration was really low. But remember, it only takes one really great contact to make the event successful for you. I have a lot of friends who love to attend networking events with over 100 attendees. They love to call me and invite me to attend, telling me how great these events are. I always ask how many people they actually talk with at these events and how they choose who to talk with. The answer never really surprises me. Most people tell me they talk with five to 10 people at a typical event. That means the other 90 or so people are pretty much extras in the event, right? For some reason, they never seem to like that answer. Remember, my friends, quality over quantity is always your best bet when it comes to making connections.

NEVER TOO HIGH, NEVER TOO LOW

When I started Friends of Kevin, a friend told me the biggest challenge I'd face was learning to never get too high and never get too low. As a business owner, you'll have weeks that will go incredibly well and you'll make great money, and you'll have other weeks where you'll wonder why you were ever crazy enough to start your own business. Remember, every business owner goes through these cycles. So don't let emotions take over. Stay level headed and everything will work out.

BE THANKFUL

I recently started a new habit. At the end of the day, I post three things I'm thankful for on Facebook, along with a picture. I've found this habit makes me focus on the good things that happen to me every day. I'm not going to lie to you. Some days I have to think really, really hard to find them, but they're always there. I suggest that you start this habit too and be sure to tag me in the post so I can comment on it. You'll find this is probably the best tip in the whole book, because you'll find yourself saying, "Hey, maybe this day wasn't as bad as I thought," or "Wow, I really did have a super day."

BE OPEN TO NEW OPPORTUNITIES

A friend asked me to do a networking event at his office. I have to admit, my gut feeling was to say no, because I didn't believe he had enough parking in the area. But because he's my friend, I stopped by to see him and, to my surprise, they changed the parking in the area! So now there's plenty of parking. I came really close to missing out on a great opportunity. So don't be too quick to turn down an opportunity. Give yourself a chance to check out an idea and see if you can make it work before you say no to it. It may turn out to be the best opportunity you ever had.

HOST AN EVENT

Hosting an event is a simple way to grow your network. This allows people to see you in your environment and make them feel like they know you better. The first few times you host an event, it may not be as well attended as you had hoped. But don't give up. Don't be shy about asking your friends to help you by bringing along their friends. Remember that old commercial from the seventies for shampoo? "If you tell two friends and they tell two friends and so on and so on." Soon you'll be hosting a successful event. I can tell you, it's a real challenge to start networking events. Every time I host a networking event in a new area, it's like starting over from scratch. But I can also tell you that attendance will grow quickly if you stay with it.

IT'S A MATTER OF TRUST

Besides being my favorite Billy Joel song, networking comes down to being a Matter of Trust. The larger the investment, the more risk of loss, the longer it will take to build trust. My friends own a butcher shop. If you stop in and buy a steak and don't like it (that would never happen; their steaks are awesome), you might be out $20 (I like big steaks). In the scheme of things, $20 doesn't seem like a big deal. You may be a little leery about buying that next steak, but you'll probably give them another chance to make a good impression. Now if you hire a broker to invest $5000 in the stock market and she loses half of it, that's a really big deal. It's only natural that you might stop using that broker. If you *are* that broker or that butcher, don't give up on networking. Stay out there. Show people they can trust you. Explain what you do and how it's done. Sometimes there are just bad meats or bad investments that don't work out as hoped. Rebuild the trust by networking.

IT'S OKAY TO FAIL

The only thing I hate more than failing is not having the guts to try things. The New England B2B Networking Group is going through a very rapid event expansion plan and some of the venues I've chosen haven't gone well, while others have been total home runs. I don't know how events will turn out, so I try pretty much every venue I'm offered. Not every idea you have will work and you'll suffer setbacks, but if you don't keep finding ways to grow your business, eventually you'll hit that proverbial wall and your business will suffer. So take chances and remember, it's not failure, it's another lesson learned.

THE IMPORTANCE OF PATIENCE

A guy who heard me speak about business networking two years ago called me recently. He's finally ready to start his own business and wants to attend some networking events. When I go out to speak about business networking, I'm simply trying to share my knowledge and spread the word about Friends of Kevin. If I meet a new client, that's great, but it's not my focus. Many of my friends get disappointed when they speak to a group and don't pick up any new clients. My friends, speaking to groups is about spreading the word about your business and positioning yourself as an expert in your field. People may not need your services today, but this is when you have the chance to make an impression. Take advantage of that chance and hopefully they'll reach out to you in the future when they're ready. Or they may recommend you to a friend who needs your services now. So be patient.

THERE'S NO FAST FORWARD BUTTON WITH BUSINESS NETWORKING

Throughout this book, I've said business networking is all about making connections and getting people to know, like, and trust you. My friends, there's no fast forward button with business networking. You can't skip the know, like, and trust part.

Lately, people have been sending me emails asking for 30 minutes of my time to show me a sales video, because they know once I see it, I'll definitely want to be part of their "great opportunity." If you've never met me, how do you know I'll be interested? Moreover, because you don't know me, how do you know we'll like each other and be able to work together? See what happens when you skip the relationship building part of business networking? It just doesn't work. At least one guy was honest with me and said "Look, you have a ton of contacts. If even 10 percent of them joined your team under this multi-level marketing venture, I'd be rich."

Don't fast forward and assume that we'll know, like, and trust each other. Network with people, learn what they do and what they like, and convince them they can trust you and your product. Show them how the opportunity would benefit them. I strongly recommend that you get to know people before you attempt to sell to them.

VOLUNTEER

One of the best ways to network and showcase your skills is by volunteering to serve on a committee or board. Only volunteer if you care about the cause and don't walk in passing out your business cards. If you're volunteering just to get business, members of the group will see right through you and will probably ask you to leave. I've made some great friends and connections through volunteering because I was able to showcase my skills and passion for the causes I committed to helping. It takes time to build those relationships, so only volunteer to make a difference, not to make money. Gaining business may be a pleasant side effect to volunteering but should not be your goal. Volunteering is also a great way for job seekers to find work. Many of my friends have volunteered for nonprofits and been offered jobs. Remember the previously discussed karma bank?

DOES YOUR MOTHER KNOW YOU DO THAT?

I'm amazed that my friends never ask their family and friends for referrals. I ran into an old friend last week and asked about his brother. He said his brother was doing great and had a cool job in Boston. When I asked what his brother was doing, he shrugged and said, "I have no idea but I think he likes it." This, my friends, goes into the epic fail category. Whether you're a job seeker or business owner, reach out to everyone you know and explain to them what you do and how they can help you. I learned this lesson a few years ago from one of my older friends. He asked me about my business and honestly, I gave a quick answer without going into much detail. He smiled at me and said, "Son, I've been on this earth for 78 years, and I have a few friends who may like to meet you." So we spent some time talking about my business, and sure enough, he gave me a handful of great people to talk to. So don't dismiss your family and friends. As I like to say, if your momma won't refer you, how can you expect anyone else to?

CO-WORKERS

I'm often amazed by people who work in larger companies who never network with their co-workers. They may eat lunch and chat every day with the people in their own department but never connect with people in the company's other departments. You don't have to be best friends or go away on vacations together, but you should connect professionally. This may help you get promoted or transferred if another position opens up. They may also be willing to help you find your next position through their own outside connections, if you should lose or decide to change your job.

THINGS TO CONSIDER BEFORE YOU JOIN A MORNING NETWORKING GROUP

Are you a morning person? A lot of my friends simply do not like getting out of bed in the morning. If you're like them, joining a group and making a commitment to be there every week may not be the best idea for you.

What's the location of the group? Many people try to join the biggest morning networking group they can find, thinking it will result in more referrals. That may be true, but are you committed to making that commute each week? I have many friends who commute over an hour to get to their meeting.

Next, think about the day of the week the group meets. Many of my friends take a three-day weekend all summer long, so joining a Friday group is probably not a great idea for them.

Also, try out various groups before you join. I'm a huge fan of morning networking groups. One thing I like about them is that each group has its own personality. Some groups can be very laid back and others can be strict. Look for a group that fits your personality. You should also consider your sphere of influence. For example, if you're a home stager, meet with the realtor, mortgage person, and home builder in your group to see how well you get along and to see if they're open to working with you. This is probably the most important thing to do before you join any morning networking group. If your sphere of influence doesn't plan on using you, if they already have long standing contacts in your field, then you may want to search for a different group.

Lastly, ask about what happened to the last person who had your seat in the group. Why did he or she leave? If possible, talk to that person and ask. I understand that this can be a little awkward sometimes. Things don't work out because of personality conflicts or because people have different approaches to business. But if you find out that several people have had the seat and left the group quickly, a red flag should go flying. You should find out why, and if you can't, you may want to find a different group.

BE SEEN AS A CONNECTOR

Most of you know I make a living out of positioning myself as a connector. I'm proud that complete strangers contact me when they need something. I think we all know that one person who seems to know everyone. Strive to be that person. Let me tell you, it's a great feeling when you get to call someone out of the blue and tell them you have a referral for them. I can assure you that the simple act of connecting two people will go a long way towards keeping you in the minds of others and helping you stand out with your network.

SPEAK TO GROUPS

The first time I went out to speak about networking, I was really scared. I kept thinking they wouldn't like me or care about what I had to say. So I was surprised by how much fun I had and how well my presentation went. Everyone has an expertise they can speak about. Take that chance and come out of your shell to show people you're an expert in your field. You may not hit it out of the park on your first try, but I promise, it does get easier the more often you do it. Speaking engagements give you a different venue in which to make connections. Not to mention, it's a great skill to have and a résumé booster.

DON'T OVERSELL YOURSELF

When you're first starting out or if business is slow, it can be tempting to oversell yourself, take on jobs you're not prepared to handle, and then fail miserably. This is a really bad decision, my friends. If you're honest and say, "I'm sorry, that's not my area of expertise," the person will respect that and hopefully call you in the future. If you take on a job you're not prepared for and mess it up, not only will that person be upset with you, he or she might tell others about how you failed and discourage his or her friends from doing business with you. Think about this the next time you're tempted to take on a job you're not prepared for. Is it really worth risking your reputation?

IT'S ALL ABOUT THEM

A friend always tells me, "Kevin, people want to know what's in it for them." It doesn't matter how cool your product or service is, if it's not going to improve their life or business, you'll have a hard time convincing people to purchase it. For example, I host in-person networking events to help my clients grow their businesses. If I meet you at another event, I'll ask you how often you attend networking events. If you say you hardly ever attend them because you can't stand them, I probably won't tell you how great my networking events are. You probably won't attend my event, so I won't waste your time trying to convince you how great my product and I are. So always focus your pitch on the needs of the potential client and not yourself.

INTROVERTS NEED TO NETWORK TOO

A lot of people tell me they're too introverted or shy to attend networking events. But if you want your business to thrive, in-person networking is essential. So you need to get out of your comfort zone and just do it. To make it easier, my introverted and shy friends have given me a few tips for you. First, focus on just one person at a time. Introverts do better with one-on-one conversations, so instead of trying to get into a circle of people, find someone who's alone and say hello. That person might be an introvert too and be very grateful! Ask questions about his or her business. People love to be listened to and introverts are good listeners. Most importantly, keep going to the events. They'll get easier over time, partly because you're practicing and partly because you'll see many of the same people and you'll start getting to know them and getting comfortable around them. That's how you build relationships, and that's what networking is all about.

BE AN ADVOCATE

People love to use me as their reference. I always go out of my way to be their advocate and tell a story about why people should do business with them. Be an advocate for your clients. It will go a long way towards building your relationships with them. When I meet people, I tell them I run this awesome networking group, but it's much more powerful when my friends tell them the group is good and they should get involved. We all need advocates, so be one for your clients.

NETWORK FOR YOUR CLIENTS

The best networkers I know attend events to meet people who may be able to help their clients. Sure, they hope to meet a new client or two for themselves, but that's not their focus. Helping a client feels great and it's good for business too.

BUILD ALLIANCES

By building alliances with people in professions that are related to your field, you're opening yourself up to many great referral opportunities. An alliance might consist of a real estate agent, a mortgage broker, an insurance agent, a home inspector, and various residential contractors. Think about the people you work with and consider inviting the ones you like and trust to create an alliance. For the alliance to work, everyone in it has to be willing to pass referrals to the other members. Please don't join an alliance unless you're willing to pass referrals.

ADD VALUE

One of my LinkedIn contacts emails me networking articles a few times a month. His emails simply say "I saw this article and thought of you. Hope all is well." He asks for nothing in return. This is a great way to add value to a relationship. He's definitely building his "know, like, and trust factor." If I need to hire or refer someone in his line of work, you can bet he'll be at the top of my list. Think about ways you can add value to your connections. It could be as simple as offering to introduce them to one of your contacts. I highly recommend this simple tip to help you grow your business.

I'M GOING TO START MY OWN NETWORKING GROUP

Good luck to you, let me know how it works out for you. You have to understand, I do this for a living. Most people think it's a piece of cake. You simply go on Facebook or LinkedIn, post an invitation, and everyone just magically appears. I wish it were that easy, my friends. But it's not a Field of Dreams and they won't come if you build it. You have to constantly remind them. Just posting doesn't always work. There are follow up emails, voicemails, Facebook messages and then more reminding after that. It's also important to find the right people to attend. You always want to have a good mix of professions. So go ahead and try, but please be prepared. It's a lot of work. Do you want help? Email me at Kevin@friendsofkevin.com. I'll be glad to help.

DON'T FORGET YOUR ROOTS

I'm very proud of the fact that I grew up in the Acre section of Lowell, MA. It's not the most affluent section of the city. There were a lot of big families from different backgrounds. I learned so much from living in a multi-cultural neighborhood. This helps me now because I deal with many different types of people with different levels of success and varying styles of business management. No matter what level of success I achieve, I always do my best to remember my roots and to never think I'm too important to find time to volunteer or help out a friend in need. This is true for growing your business too. Sure, as business grows, you must evolve and make some changes. But remember where you were when you started and who helped you get your start. Keep those roots strong and you and your business will keep growing.

SOMETIMES IT'S AS SIMPLE AS WISHING SOMEONE A HAPPY BIRTHDAY

Last week I received my daily LinkedIn recap email and I noticed that it was a friend's birthday. This guy always goes out of his way to endorse me on LinkedIn, so I wanted to take a moment to thank him and wish him a happy birthday. He sent me back the nicest email I've ever received, thanking me for taking the time to wish him a happy birthday. I have to be honest, I was having a super stressful day, but his email made me realize that everything was going to be okay. So take the time to wish your friends a happy birthday. It just might make your day.

WHY YOU SHOULD ATTEND HOLIDAY OPEN HOUSES

The holidays can be crazy busy for most of us. It's hard to make every event you're invited to. But this is why I want you to make every effort to attend. My friends get really excited about their open houses. They always tell me, "Kevin, the event will be awesome because I invited 100 people and I'm sure they'll all attend." We all know things will come up and many people won't be able to make it. So go and have a Mountain Dew and a few cookies. I think we can all find a few minutes to spare even during this busy time of year. Come on people, it's the holidays. Live a little and tell them it was an awesome event, because that's what friends do.

NO ONE IS BETTER THAN YOU

I was talking with a friend last week. I hadn't seen him at an event in a while. When I asked him why he stopped coming, he said it was because the people in the room were better than him. I must admit, I was at a loss for words, and if you know me, you know that never happens. I was quick to jump in and correct him. Please listen carefully: Nobody is better than you. They might have a fancier title than you, they might have on a nicer suit or drive a fancier car, but they'll never be better than you. So please never ever think that. Just like you, they're at a networking event trying to grow their business.

ONE EVENT ISN'T ENOUGH

Recently, I asked a woman to attend one of my networking events. She said she tried a networking event once and didn't get anything out of it and it was a waste of 45 minutes. I have to be honest, it was tough not to burst out laughing, but I decided it was probably better to smile and say I understood. This is an extreme example, but it does happen. People attend a few events, and when they don't get any business, they say networking doesn't work for their type of business and stop attending. Networking works for all types of businesses. Just like any other endeavor, practice makes perfect. You wouldn't try to play a sport for the first time and then give up if you weren't perfect at it, would you? No, you'd keep going back, keep honing your skill, and before you knew it, you'd be good at it! Keep going to those networking events. You'll get better at talking about yourself and your business and you'll build relationships with people who'll help you grow your business while you help them grow theirs.

Kevin Willett

TIME MANAGEMENT

SCHEDULE YOUR NETWORKING EVENTS LIKE APPOINTMENTS

If you're reading this book, you know that networking is essential to growing your business. Many people never make networking a priority. They attend events only if it's convenient and often look for reasons to skip events. Treat networking events like appointments and schedule them in your calendar at the beginning of the month. If someone asked to meet you at a time when you already had an appointment, wouldn't you suggest another time? Of course you would. But many people will skip a networking event if a potential client asks to meet them at the time when the event is scheduled. Try to do both before you just back out of the event. Or try to meet before the event and then bring the potential client along as your guest and introduce him or her to people at the event. It will make a great first impression.

MAKE TIME FOR YOURSELF

I struggle to balance work and personal time. As a business owner, you can always be doing something else to grow your business. You can find yourself working seven days a week and more hours than you wish to admit. Trust me on this one. You need to set boundaries. You have to pick a firm start and stop point to your days and plan for days off; otherwise you'll become the saddest successful person in the world. The balancing act can be challenging for business owners who have a home office. Think it about it. If you wake up at 4 a.m., it's easy to jump online and start working when you have a home office. But would you shower and head into a regular office at 4 a.m.? Probably not, because you'd look silly getting in that early. I've learned to take baby steps. I started by not working on Sundays past 3 p.m. and I try to stop every night at 7 p.m. Guess what? I find I'm more productive working less hours, because I'm not falling asleep at the keyboard or losing my concentration. Give this a try and let me know how it works out.

STOP WAITING FOR THINGS TO BE PERFECT

For the last few months, I've been going back and forth with a gentleman who's interested in attending some of my networking events. He always has a reason to wait to start networking. He wants to make sure everything's perfect so that he'll make a really great first impression, because his brand is important to him. I agree that your brand is one of your biggest assets and you need to make a positive first impression. But that doesn't mean things have to be perfect. So the last time he called, I said, "Hey, how's business going for you?" He said business was horrible and he was having a really hard time finding new clients. I politely told him that we'd been speaking for three months now, and each time, he had a reason not to attend an event. First he wanted to redo his business cards because he didn't like the shade of blue he used for them, then he didn't like the font used on his brochures, and now he's redoing his website, which may take three months or so. I said, "Did you ever think that maybe things are good enough? I have to be honest, most people won't notice the changes you plan on making with your cards and brochures, but you're using these changes to delay the success of your business." Of course, this wasn't a great conversation for either of us, but he did agree that it was more important to start networking now than to wait for things to be perfect. My friends, things will never be perfect. You'll always want to tweak your marketing materials. But chances are they're good enough for you to start networking now.

IT'S OKAY TO ASK FOR HELP

Hello, my name is Kevin and I'm a control freak. Sadly, most business owners are control freaks until they realize that you simply cannot do it all yourself. I have some incredible plans for the New England B2B Networking Group, but to accomplish them, I need to let go of some things and let other people help me. I always ask myself whether a task helps me make money. If the answer is no, I delegate it. By letting go and not trying to do it all myself, I've been able to grow my business in ways I never thought possible. I understand this is a huge issue for most of us, because our business is our baby and we think nobody can do things as well as we can or they'll mess things up and hurt our brand. My friends, you need to choose great people and have faith that everything will be okay.

DON'T SPREAD YOURSELF TOO THIN

Most days, I think I'm Superman and I can do everything and attend every event. Then I realize I don't have any superpowers. Don't fall in to the trap of overbooking yourself. I see so many people do this and end up letting people down, because they have trouble getting things done on time. Spreading yourself too thin will do more harm than good.

TAKE CONTROL

You have to take control of your life if you want to be successful. I like being in control of everything, but it's not easy for a lot of people. Think about how you're spending your time and who you're spending it with. How is that affecting your business? It's easy to let busywork take up your time and make you feel productive when you're not really accomplishing anything that will build your reputation, attract clients, or bring in money. So pay careful attention to how you spend your time. You may even want to write a log of how you spend your time for a day or two. Breaks are important for your well being, so I'm not suggesting you give those up. But pay attention to what you're doing between the breaks. You may be surprised at how much time is spent on unproductive busywork.

MEASURING THE ROI ON BUSINESS NETWORKING

I do realize that I told you not to give up on networking, and I meant it. But you do need to measure the ROI (return on investment) from the various groups you're a member of. When you first start your business, a large portion of your sales may come from one particular networking group. As your business and reputation grow, that may change. This is why it's very important to track where your referrals are coming from and the results of those referrals every year to determine whether you should renew your membership to a particular group. When you're making this calculation, factor in the cost of membership and the cost of your time to attend the events, as well as any meetings for coffee to follow up. You may be very surprised by the results. Again, please don't give up on networking. It may just be time to move on to another group if the one you're currently in is no longer producing the ROI you need.

TAKE TWO DAYS OFF

I was working seven days a week for six years when my body and mind revolted and demanded a break. I was so burnt out I could barely think straight. Please learn from my experience and don't make that mistake. I know how challenging it is to launch a successful business and how important it is to put your heart and soul into it, but you need to take time off and find balance in your life. Right now, I'm running two networking groups, hosting about 25 networking events a month, writing a book, and speaking about business networking a few times a month. It's a pretty quick pace, but I force myself to carve out two days a month where I don't do any work. I've found that just taking a few days off helps my mind and body rest, which allows me to have better focus, which makes me more productive. Go to your calendar right now and block out two whole days and be sure to enjoy them.

WHY PEOPLE WHO DON'T NEED YOUR SERVICES ARE WORTH YOUR TIME

I've noticed that people often won't take the time to meet with people who don't need their services. They don't understand an important networking concept: You're not selling *to* your contacts, you're selling *through* them.

I was scheduled to meet someone who was interested in joining the group. He emailed me 30 minutes before the meeting saying he wasn't in a position to join at this time and asked me if I still wanted to meet up. To be honest, I was having a typical super crazy day and it was tempting to cancel. But I asked myself, "Is this the image you want this person to have of you?" Of course it wasn't, so I told him I appreciated his honesty, but of course I still wanted to meet with him.

It was a great meeting. We really hit it off and were able to refer some friends to each other. Now if I was silly and cancelled the appointment, I wouldn't have had that chance. So remember, although the people you meet might not need your services, they may have friends or family who do. I'm happy to be someone's second choice when it comes to networking. I have made a successful business out of being second best.

READ

The best advice I can give you is to spend a few minutes each day reading about your industry. I like to spend a few minutes each day searching twitter for #networking. I've found some awesome ideas that I've been able to share with my followers. Try to schedule in a few minutes each day to read and share articles with your friends about trends in your industry.

SUMMERTIME NETWORKING

I find that many people take the summer off from networking. I may be biased because I run two networking groups, but I'll do my best to convince you that it's a really bad idea. If you disappear for three or four months, people may believe that you went out of business, especially if you're a new business owner. Also, you've been working hard to build relationships through networking. When you take several months off from events, it can feel like you're starting over. I suggest that you find time to attend one or two events a month that you really like and find valuable to keep your name out there. If you find that you simply cannot attend events, make sure you're staying in touch with your connections through your newsletter or by emailing them.

GUARD YOUR TIME

Last week, I was scheduling a meeting with a potential client. He said any time the following week would work, because he had nothing going on. That may be true, my friends, but never admit that. It sends the wrong message. Your time is a precious resource, so treat it that way. Many people ask to meet me for coffee because they want to talk to me about "something." Sorry guys, I don't have time for vague requests. If people don't tell you why they want to see you, it's a pretty sure bet you're in for a sales pitch. Don't waste your time meeting people who can't give you a good reason to meet. You can also save time with meetings by doing them by phone or Skype. Please be respectful of your own time and that of the person you want to meet.

BEFORE EVENTS

SET NETWORKING GOALS

Way back when I first started Friends of Kevin, a woman spent about 45 minutes at one of my networking events. When I followed up with her, she said she was disappointed because nothing happened. I guess she missed the part of the book about the whole know, like, and trust thing. I asked her what she thought would happen and she said she didn't know. So I said, "Then how do you know it didn't happen?"

It's important that you set networking goals and that they're reasonable. A guy told me his goal was to attract five new clients at every event. I have to admit, I chuckled when he told me this. I asked him if he'd ever achieved that goal. He said he hadn't even come close. It's very important to set reasonable goals. When I first started going to networking events, my goal was to make three new contacts and then I could leave. Once I achieved that goal, I changed it to five new contacts. Eventually, my goal was to stay for the whole event. That may not sound like much, but I was really shy back then. So before you attend an event, set challenging but achievable goals to get the most out of your networking experience.

WHERE DO YOU BELONG?

Of course, I encourage you to always attend networking events. But you need to find events that potential clients and partners will actually be attending. Before you attend any event or join any networking group, do your due diligence to make sure you're spending your time wisely. People often call me and ask if they should attend one of my events. They're surprised when I tell them they shouldn't attend a particular event. I want you to use your time wisely and I really can't lie about it, because you'll know if it was a good use of your time.

PURCHASE A REAL NAME BADGE

I highly encourage you to spend a few dollars and purchase a name badge, rather than using the "Hello my name is" badge available at events. This is an inexpensive way to look professional. The stick-on badge that's provided to you at the door has issues. First, can people read your handwriting? You don't want to be judged on bad penmanship. These nametags rarely last through the night without curling or falling off completely. If you get a real name badge, keep it simple. Make sure we can actually read the font. Just your name, title, and business name should suffice. A small logo is acceptable if there's room. People often try to put too much information on the badge, which makes the print tiny (unless you're wearing a billboard, and that's definitely a turnoff). Tiny print creates an awkward situation when we have to stand two inches away from you to try and read it.

REGISTRATION ETIQUETTE FOR EXCLUSIVE NETWORKING EVENTS

Networking events are either exclusive or open. Exclusive events are often limited by industry or by the number of attendees. Only register for these events if you're sure you can attend, and notify the host immediately if something comes up and you can't make it. I host industry exclusive events as part of the New England B2B Networking Group and it's really challenging when people fail to show up. I try to invite people who I believe may be able to do business together or be great referral sources for the other attendees, so if one person is missing, it can impact the effectiveness of the event. Throughout this book, I'll ask the same question: "Is that the image you want people to have of you?" If you fail to show up to an exclusive networking event, the message you're sending is that you're not reliable. My friends, nobody wants to refer someone who isn't reliable.

OPEN NETWORKING EVENTS

Open networking events are open to everyone and are usually well attended. The hardest part of running networking events is getting people to register. Many people wait until the last minute to sign up to make sure they can attend. I respect this, but let me explain to you what goes on behind the curtain. When I'm hosting an event, I think about the size of the venue and how many people will fit in there comfortably. Some venues can hold 20 and some can hold 100. So if the venue holds 20, I invite people until I have 20 registered and then I stop, because I don't want to have 30 people attend a venue that only holds 20. So if an event has limited registration, waiting to register could mean missing out on the event.

As a friend of mine always says, people want to know what's in it for them. Here's what's in it for you: As the host, I review all of the registered attendees so I can do my best to introduce them to potential clients and partners. Also, many attendees review the list and ask me to introduce them to people they don't know. So by not registering, you're missing out on the chance to make those connections.

Lastly, I want to talk about what I call networking math. For open events, I find 30 is the magic number. If people see that 30 people have registered, they feel like everyone is going and they want to go too. If I have 20 or less, they feel that it's going to be a small crowd, so they'll often skip it. So you're doing the host a huge favor by registering early.

RESEARCH ATTENDEES

I have a friend who'll call me the day of a networking event and ask about every person who's attending, so he knows who to look for at the event. You might think this is a bit extreme, but it works for him. His goal is to meet great people who may be able to help his clients. I encourage you to research the attendees as a way to stand out at a networking event. Which of these scenarios do you like better? Someone walks up to you at an event and asks you who you are and what you do.

Or someone walks up to you and says "Hello Joe, I'm glad to meet you. How's the printing business going for you?" I think we can agree that the second approach will make a much better first impression, especially because so few people will actually take the time to do it. Try this out at your next networking event. I'm sure you'll be pleasantly surprised by the results.

YOU LEFT HOME WITHOUT YOUR BUSINESS CARDS?

I was meeting with a potential client and one of my friends was sitting at the next table. He leaned over and said "Hey Kevin, give me one of your business cards. My friend wants to learn more about your group." Guess what? I didn't have any cards with me. If I wasn't so embarrassed, it would've been funny, because the three of them — and it felt like everyone else in the room — all seemed to gasp. Kevin Willett, the professional networker, the guy who wrote this book and does all those videos about networking tips, has no cards with him! Epic fail, my friends. So when you're done reading this tip, put the book down and put some cards in your wallet, purse, bags, and car so you never have to feel as unprepared as I did that day.

DRESS APPROPRIATELY

I always suggest to my friends that they dress for the job they want, not the job they have. When you're at a networking event, people are judging you on your appearance. You don't need a $5,000 suit to look successful or worthy of my business. But, if your shirt has wrinkles in it or your suit doesn't fit correctly, people may judge you as being sloppy or not having the ability to pay attention to details. If you're not sure what to wear to an event, call the host and ask, because you can look silly and stuffy wearing a suit to a BBQ networking event.

Let me close out this tip with a story. A few summers ago, one of my friends came to a networking event wearing shorts and a company t-shirt. The first time he did it, I let it go, but the second time, I asked him if he ever watched Sesame Street when he was a kid. He gave me a puzzled look and said, "Sure, why do you ask?" I said, "Do you remember which one of these things isn't like the other? It's you, dude! You're the only one in the room wearing shorts." I know wearing a suit to summer events can be tough, but it's important to look professional at all times.

BREATH MINTS

Always carry breath mints when you're meeting people. Nothing leaves a worse first impression than bad breath. I don't want to know that you had too much coffee today or garlic for lunch. You don't want the odor coming out of your mouth to distract from the words you're saying. If someone offers you a mint, they're trying to send you a message, so please be grateful and take it.

USE THE BUDDY PLAN

A client told me that she struggles with networking events, because she has a hard time walking up to people she doesn't know and introducing herself. So I suggested she use what I call "The Buddy Plan" and go with a friend. This can be a great way to feel comfortable at an event. When you do this, it can be tempting to just stand together all night in the corner. That's not networking! You have to mix and mingle with others. So if you're shy, try not to go with someone who's as shy as you.

I personally like to go to events with my friends and spend the whole night introducing them around. My friends are always extremely appreciative. I always smile because I also receive a lot of benefits from helping. First, my friends are thankful, and second, I get a chance to meet more people who think I'm a nice guy for helping my friends. Typically, when I'm at an event, people will ask me if I can introduce them too, so I'm often helping two or three people at each event.

If you don't have a buddy, call or email the host and ask if he or she knows anyone who can help. Most groups can pair you with one of their regulars to introduce you around. If you come to one of my events, just come over and stand next to me and I'll take care of you for the event.

EAT BEFORE YOU ATTEND AN EVENT

Unless you're attending a dinner, always eat before an event. People often say to me, "Kevin, there's free food.

Why wouldn't I take advantage of that?" Have you ever tried to talk with someone who has a drink in one hand, a plate in the other, and a mouth full of food? How did that work out for you? It simply doesn't. If you need to eat, grab a quick bite and get back to the reason you attended the event, to network. I always joke with my friends and say if you think you may have set a new world record for shrimp consumption at a networking event, then you're doing something wrong.

PROMOTE NETWORKING EVENTS YOU PLAN ON ATTENDING

Most people think it's easy to run a business networking event. I wish they were right. It's not the field of dreams they think it is. I don't just invite people and they attend. I have to follow up with them with emails and text messages and remind them. If you want to be my best friend, help me promote my events. Helping build the attendance benefits not just me, but you and the entire group as well. It creates chances to meet friends of friends and make new connections. I always tell people I run a really awesome networking group, but they might think I'm just saying that because it benefits me. When you share my events, you're helping me raise awareness of the group, while at the same time endorsing me to your friends and letting them know that, yeah, it really *is* an awesome networking group. For those who do that, I'm very grateful.

JUST GO ALREADY

If I had a dollar for every time someone told me, "I've been meaning to come to one of your events," I'd be writing this book from my own private island. It's okay to be apprehensive about attending events, but if you want your business to succeed, you can't use that as an excuse not to attend. I remember when I first started networking. I kept saying I'd go to the next networking event, but on the day of the event I'd find some really good reason not to go, like being too tired. When I finally did attend, I was proud of myself for getting out of my comfort zone. I want you to stop reading for a minute and register for a networking event. Be sure to add it to your calendar, and when the time comes, push yourself to go if you have to, so you can get over your fear of networking. It worked for me and it will work for you.

Kevin Willett

DURING EVENTS

ARRIVE EARLY FOR NETWORKING EVENTS

The hardest part of hosting a networking event is the 15 minutes before the event begins. We hosts can get nervous thinking nobody's going to show up. If you arrive about 10 minutes early, the host will appreciate it. For myself, having someone to talk with takes my mind off of wondering how many people will show up and whether a good time will be had by all. What is in it for you? First, you can often spend some quality time with the host. I can only speak for myself, but when I have 10 minutes to talk with someone before an event, I usually end up introducing them to a lot of people simply because their story is fresh on my mind. Second, it allows you more one-on-one time with other early arrivers. Also, the host often needs help with some last minute preparations, so being that helpful person will go a long way towards building your relationship with the host. I'd like to thank everyone who shows up early for my events. Thanks for keeping me calm and entertained.

IF YOU CAN'T ARRIVE EARLY, ARRIVE ON TIME

I encourage you to treat networking events like appointments and arrive on time. I understand that this may not always be possible due to the location of the event or unexpected traffic. But if you arrive late to every event, people might believe that you'll show up late for appointments you make with them as well, and nobody likes their time wasted. So do your best to arrive on time. It shows that you take your commitments seriously.

QUALITY OVER QUANTITY 2

I used to know a gentleman who would attend events and just walk up to people and hand them his card. One night I stopped him and said "Why do you pass out your cards to everyone in the room?" He replied, "So you'll call me when you need me." I said, "I'll never call you, because I don't know you or what you do, so please take your card back. Next time, take a moment to introduce yourself and tell me a little bit about what you do and then maybe we can work up to doing business together." He frowned at me, grabbed his card, and hasn't spoken to me since.

You'll run into a number of "card pushers" at events. Their simple goal is to make sure that everyone in the room leaves with their card. My friends, when it comes to networking events, quality is always more important than quantity. You can't meet everyone at a networking event, so don't try. It comes across as though you're running a campaign to be the president of the United States, trying to shake as many hands as possible. Instead, focus on having a few really good conversations with people who can help you and with people you can help. Those are the people you'll build the "know, like, and trust" factor with.

ARE YOU DOMINATING THE CONVERSATION?

After I meet with someone, I try to evaluate how well I explained the benefits of my networking groups. Sometimes, guys, I want a do-over, because I realize I did a horrible job. It's important to understand the person's needs before you pitch your business. As you know, I host in-person networking events and I also promote my clients through social media. If I'm out at an event and I ask someone if she comes to events all the time and she says, "God no, I hate going to events," then it would be rather silly of me to tell her about my in-person events. I'd be better off talking about my social media promotion. God gave you two ears and one mouth for a reason. Try to listen twice as much as you speak.

BE POSITIVE

Have you ever met with someone who was negative about everything? You ask him how his day was and he says it was horrible. You ask her how business is going and she says it was her worst year ever. Now why would you possibly want to do business with a person like this, when you can't be sure she'll be in business next week? Please don't be negative when you're speaking with potential clients and business partners. It's a huge turnoff. Please don't use networking events to complain about your life. Remember to always be positive. Attitude is everything when you're trying to sell yourself and your work.

Kevin Willett

THE BIGGEST NETWORKING MISTAKE YOU'LL EVER MAKE

People often say to me, "Kevin, please only introduce me to people who have a need and the means to pay for my goods and services." My friends, that is the biggest mistake you can ever make when networking. Remember that you're not selling *to* your network, you're selling *through* them. I'd like to use myself as an example. My needs as a business owner are pretty straightforward. I need a phone, Wi-Fi, a computer, Mountain Dew, and pizza. Many business owners would totally dismiss me because I probably don't have a need for their goods or services. But I'm a professional networker with over 20,000 connections (and growing). *Now* do you want to network with me? Don't dismiss anyone. You never know where your next referral is coming from.

TO REDUCE YOUR FEAR OF NETWORKING, FOCUS ON GIVING RATHER THAN RECEIVING

I've found that when I focus my efforts on helping people connect at networking events, I always have a great night and end up signing a new client or picking up a few really great contacts. When you focus on helping other people, it takes the pressure off, because you're not trying to sell anything, you're just there as a resource. I've seen people fear networking simply because they don't know what to say, or because they struggle to find that line between trying to gain new clients and coming across as pushy and aggressive. The next time you go to an event, ask everyone you meet how you can help them or who you can introduce them to who might help them grow their business. This simple approach will help you stand out at networking events. Be prepared to answer that question for yourself when someone asks you.

BE APPROACHABLE AND SMILE

Have you ever walked into a networking event and nobody in the room would make eye contact with you? That has to be one of the most awkward feelings in the world. People want to feel welcomed when they arrive. So smile at them and say hello and welcome them into your conversation. I've made some great contacts just by being approachable and being the first person to talk to somebody new at a networking event. I have a friend who always talks about how I stopped in the middle of a story at an event and waved him over to listen and meet my friends because I knew he was new. We became friends that night because I showed him some love.

BE ABLE TO CLEARLY STATE WHAT YOU DO AND WHO A GOOD REFERRAL IS FOR YOU

This sounds pretty easy and straight forward, but often when I ask someone who a great referral would be for them, they tell me anyone with a pulse. My friends, we're back in the epic fail category. If you tell me financial planners and CPAs are great contacts for you, I can start helping you right away. There's an expression in networking that "everyone turns into no one simply because people don't know where to start." Here's an example. If you're a CPA and you tell me everyone is a potential client, I'll agree with you, but I probably won't ever give you a referral. If you tell me you specialize in helping people and businesses that have tax issues, then I'll know to refer you whenever I hear of someone with that issue. Remember, the more specific you are, the easier it is to refer you. I have a friend who's a painter. If you ask who a good referral is, he'll tell you the exact size and type of the house he wants to paint, including how many windows the house has. His description makes you visualize this house. If he said anyone who needs painting done, would that make you visualize anything? If it would, it's probably not too pretty.

BE PRESENT AND PAY ATTENTION TO ME

Have you ever been talking to someone and the whole time she was either looking at her phone or scanning the room to see if there was anyone cooler than you to talk to? My friends, this behavior is simply rude and disrespectful. People have stopped talking to me mid-sentence and run over to someone else in the room. What do you think the chances are that I'll refer them? I have to be honest, I've done this myself. I don't mean to be rude. I suffer from a short attention span and I get distracted without even trying. So I've learned to move my body so that I'm facing a wall when I'm talking with someone. This helps eliminate most of the distractions for me. Do whatever you have to in order to give the person you're speaking with 100 percent of your attention. Also, if you're expecting an important call, mention it to the person you're talking with so he'll know you're not just being rude.

THE BEST ICE BREAKER IS "HELLO"

Sometimes networking events feel like high school dances. You're looking at someone, and she's looking at you, but neither of you makes the first move, so you end up leaning against the wall with your friends all night. How about you walk over to the person and smile and say hello? You came to the event to meet people and so did they, so what are you waiting for?

DON'T WAIT, INITIATE

That's right, stop waiting for people to talk to you. Walk right on over and say hello, especially to the person standing alone. This happened to me years ago, when I was just starting out in business. A friend invited me to a men's dinner for a local nonprofit. I arrived early and found myself standing alone, drinking a coke. I knew no one there and nobody came over to talk to me. At the time, I was way too shy to walk over to a group of successful business owners because I thought, why would they want to talk to me? My friends, that was the longest 30 minutes of my life, waiting for my friend to arrive. So please don't wait. Initiate a conversation with that poor guy standing alone. I can assure you that he'll appreciate your kindness. I never realized why I was so crazy about making sure nobody's alone at my events until I wrote this tip. I guess I don't want anyone feeling like I did that night.

DON'T JUDGE ME

It's tempting to judge others quickly based upon their appearance or occupation. In networking, this is a rookie mistake. While many of the people you meet may never be your client, they may know people who would be great clients for you. Remember, you're not selling *to* your network, you're selling *through* them. You might think there's no way that a person who does that for a living would know someone who'd be a great client for you. Take a chance and be friendly to everyone you meet. They might just surprise you.

ASK OPEN-ENDED QUESTIONS

Many people don't like to network because they're just not comfortable with small talk. We've all had those painful conversations where we exchange one-word answers. When I'm talking with someone, I always try to find at least one question that will make the person smile and open up to me.

Let me give you an example. I was talking with a CPA at a networking event and, my friends, it was painful. I asked him three questions and he answered each with only one or two words. So finally, I asked him if he ever uncovered anyone stealing. Oh my God, his eyes almost jumped out his head and he went into this rather long and involved story about how he figured out a bookkeeper had been stealing money for years from her employer. I've been friends with him ever since, because I invested the time to connect with him. I could have just walked away, saying to myself, this guy has no personality. But I would have missed an opportunity to make a great friendship.

So when you meet people, ask yourself one question: What would be important to this person? Then ask them about that. If you're not sure what to ask, simply ask what they feel is their biggest accomplishment. You'll learn a lot about someone from the answer.

HOW ARE YOU DIFFERENT?

Let me ask you a question. How are you different from everyone else who does what you do? You provide better customer service, correct? Ninety-five percent of people will use that as the reason they're different. Have you ever heard anyone say their customer service is really lousy? If you're going to use this as your reason, then follow it up with a story about how you saved the day for a client. But it would be better to put some time into figuring out what truly makes you different from your competition. How are your product's benefits different from similar products? Is your company culture/personality different from the competition? Maybe your costs are what set you apart? Have these answers ready and stand out at your next event.

BE CONSCIOUS OF THE AMOUNT OF TIME YOU SPEND WITH SOMEONE AT AN EVENT

Have you ever gone to a networking event and spent the whole night talking to one person? I see this happen all the time, and the person is usually a friend. This is a real balancing act. It's important to catch up with old friends, but please say hello, keep it brief, and make plans to meet for coffee at a later date. This will give you time to meet new people. I do my best to connect with a few people at each event. If the conversation is going well, I ask them if we can meet for coffee so I can learn more about them. You may meet people who are fascinating to you, but they may not feel the same way. Asking them to meet you for coffee gives them and you a chance to meet other people at the event. I've had the unpleasant experience of having people talk to me all night because they simply didn't know anyone else there. I did feel bad for them, but there were other people at the event I wanted to say hello to, so please don't be that clingy person.

NO SEX, RELIGION, OR POLITICS PLEASE

A newcomer to one of my networking events handed me his phone as soon as he walked in so I could read a dirty joke off of it. Now that is not the way to make a great first impression. My friends, we all have our views, but if you're at a business networking event, please keep them to yourself. Two guys at a recent event were arguing over a political issue to the point I had to ask them to stop. What do you think the other people in the room thought of them? Is that the image they were hoping for? Probably not. I've seen so many people lose business over their political views. Is it really that important to you? Please don't offend anyone by making fun of their viewpoints or arguing with them.

LOOK FOR A COMMON BOND

Most of my best clients have come to me because we share a common bond. It might be something as simple as our belief in the importance of fighting hunger in our community. Always look to find that common bond to connect with people on a personal level. As we've discussed many times, we do business with people we know, like, and trust. Please understand that we may not do business right away. People I served on boards with years ago have reconnected with me to get involved in my networking groups all because we have the same passions.

HOW TO ENTER A CONVERSATION

I have to be honest, I really struggled with this when I first started networking. It was really overwhelming for me. I'd walk into a room and see all of these people standing together talking, and I didn't know if it was okay to walk over and join them. I'd end up looking for the person standing alone and talk with him. Well, I eventually found a way to join those conversations.

When I come across a group of people, I position myself so that I'm looking directly at the person speaking, hoping he or she will make eye contact with me and invite me to join the conversation. Sometimes the conversation will shift and someone else will be carrying the discussion, so I shift my body so I can see the new speaker. If he or she doesn't let me in, I simply move on to the next group. Don't be disappointed if you're not asked to join the conversation. Some people simply don't know any better.

Recently, I learned an important tip about entering conversations. If two people are standing face to face, they're probably having a closed conversation and don't want to be disturbed. If they're standing side by side, then it's okay to approach them. I guess we're always learning new tips.

HOW TO EXIT A CONVERSATION

Many of my friends struggle with how to exit a conversation without feeling like they're hurting the person's feelings. Let me start by telling you what not to say. Don't say you have to go to the restroom and then start talking to someone else. This happened to me a few months ago and I was tempted to walk over to the person and say, "Hey, the restrooms are in the back if you need them," but we know that would be pretty childish. Don't say you're going to grab some food, because they'll probably follow you to the food line and try to talk with you while you're eating, and that can be awkward. Also, never say you're going to grab a drink, because they might follow you to the bar, and once you start drinking with someone, chances are you'll be together for the whole event.

I suggest you try something like this: "I know you didn't come here to just talk with me, so I'll let you go so you can meet other people." Now you've made it about them, so it doesn't come across as though you think they're boring and want to get away from them. Give it a try at your next networking event.

DON'T DRINK AND NETWORK

I know my friends hate the fact that I don't allow alcohol at my networking events, but I'm never going to change my mind about this. I believe drinking at networking events is always a very bad idea. You might think having one drink loosens you up and makes you more fun to network with. But the second drink could loosen you up to the point where you say something inappropriate that will wreck your reputation. My friends, you just have to trust me on this one. I've seen so many embarrassing things happen, to the point where some people never go to another event because they're too ashamed to come back. Now is that drink really worth the risk?

RELAX

The best advice I can give you is to relax and be yourself. I have many friends who get really nervous when they attend events. They're afraid they won't know anyone there or they won't know what to talk about. Just be yourself and don't try too hard. People will like you and many will approach you and help you be successful at the event.

FIRM HANDSHAKE

I recognize that there may be some cultural issues regarding touching or eye contact that may come into play here, but for this tip we'll assume there are no cultural issues. Think about the last person who shook your hand with a firm handshake and made eye contact with you. What did you think of that person? People who do that strike me as being confident, so they gain a little bit of respect from me right away. Now let's flip the coin over. Someone walks up to you, gives you a weak handshake, mumbles, and looks at the floor. How do you feel about that person? People who do that strike me as having no confidence in themselves or their business. I'm sorry, my friends, but most people won't want to do business with someone who isn't confident. So when you meet someone, give him a firm handshake and a smile, look him in the eyes, and tell him you're happy to meet him.

BODY LANGUAGE

Have you ever talked with someone who was standing with his arms folded across his chest or, as I like to call it, in the *I Dream of Jeannie* position? How approachable did he seem? This position makes people appear defensive and not open to listening to what others have to say. More people will approach you if you keep your arms uncrossed. When you're speaking with someone at an event, stand up straight. Slouching makes you look unsure of yourself. Fidgeting, toe tapping, and constantly looking around makes you look uncomfortable. Maintain eye contact so that you appear interested, but don't stare. That just makes you look creepy. Standing tall, offering a firm handshake, and focusing on the person you're talking with exudes confidence.

SELL YOUR FRIENDS

No, I don't mean you should try to sell your friends for money. I mean you should talk them up at a networking event. I have a friend who's a wedding photographer. I introduce her as the wedding photographer who can take that one special shot that captures the beauty of the bride. It still makes her blush, but it's better than saying, "This is my friend. She's a wedding photographer." The next time you're at an event, rather than saying, "This is John. He's a mechanic," try saying, "This is my mechanic, John. He's the guy I trust to keep my cars in great shape." How would you like to be introduced?

PUT YOUR PHONE AWAY

Unless you're the host of the event, please leave your phone in your pocket. More importantly, please don't take it out of your pocket to check a text message when you're talking with someone. That's simply rude. If you're anticipating a very important call, tell the person you're with that you may have to break away for a moment, as you're expecting an important call. Most people will understand. If you take out your phone in the middle of a conversation, most people will just walk away from you.

ELEVATOR SPEECH

Most people find it interesting that I hate elevator speeches. I think most of them stink. If you don't know what an elevator speech is, the definition is "a short summary used to quickly and simply define a person, profession, product, service, or organization." These speeches or pitches last approximately 30 seconds to two minutes, enough time to ride an elevator. I was at an event a few weeks ago and I asked a guy what he did. He actually slapped his shoes together and started his memorized pitch. In the middle of it, I asked him a question, just to see what he would do. He stopped, answered the question, then literally clapped his heels together and started from the beginning. As I mentioned previously, I believe you should focus your pitch on the needs of the person you're speaking with, and that's difficult with a one-size-fits-all pitch. Let me suggest a different way in the next tip.

TELL ME A STORY

When someone asks what you do, rather than saying, "I'm a realtor who goes the extra mile for my clients," add a story on to it. Try saying "I'm a realtor who goes the extra mile for my clients. Let me give you a quick example." Then tell them how you saved the day for one of your clients. Telling your story and giving real examples will help differentiate you from all the other realtors they'll meet that night.

DON'T TALK TO YOUR FRIENDS ALL NIGHT

I have a group of friends who go to all the same networking events and hang out with each other all night. Please don't do that. Not only are you getting nothing from the event, you may be damaging the event, because people may come away saying the event was lousy and the people are really cliquey.

WHO DO YOU WANT TO MEET?

When you attend one of my networking events, I'll ask you what types of professionals you'd like to meet. Here's a helpful hint: Don't tell me you want to meet everyone. I've heard it said that when you want to meet everybody, you end up meeting nobody. If you tell me you'd like to meet CPAs and lawyers, I know exactly who to introduce you to. If you say everyone, I probably won't introduce you to anyone, because your request is too vague. So please be specific.

FIND A GURU

Have you ever attended a networking event and seen that one person who just owns the room? They seem to know everyone and they always have a crowd around them laughing and having a good time. Those are the people you want to meet for coffee, so you can learn more about their networking skills.

When you ask them how they became so good at networking, many will just shrug and say something like, "It just comes naturally to me." But the longer you talk to them, the more tips they'll give you. I'm always watching the room at an event to figure out who are the leaders and connectors. I observe their skills to improve mine.

Kevin Willett

My friends, networking is like anything else you do. The more you practice, the better you become. If you can find the guru in the room, pay attention and apply what you observe to yourself.

THANK THE HOST

When was the last time you thanked the host for putting together a networking event? Most people never do. Hosting events is a lot of work and can be very stressful. Please take a moment to say thank you. The host will appreciate it.

AFTER EVENTS

HOW TO FOLLOW UP

I think Dr. Ivan Misner summed it up best when he said the best way to follow up with someone is "whichever one you are most comfortable with and can do every time the need arises." I'll add that you should do it in a timely manner. I received a LinkedIn request today from someone I met eight months ago. I recommend following up within 48 hours. Personally, I follow up by emailing people asking them to meet for coffee and also sending them a personalized LinkedIn request. I've found this combination works best for me. If you simply connect with someone on LinkedIn, unless you're staying in contact with them, the relationship will never fully develop. Take the time to follow up in person. Make that LinkedIn connection mean something. Stay in touch.

SEND A CARD TO STAND OUT

Are you looking for a way to stand out at your next networking event? Send the people you speak to a greeting card telling them how much you enjoyed meeting them. Don't send a card to everyone who attended the event, especially if you didn't talk to them. But if you made a great connection, take the time to send a card as soon as you can to help build the relationship. Remember, it's easy to send an email, and everyone does it, so send a card if you want to stand out.

CONNECT ON SOCIAL MEDIA

A guy at one of my networking events bragged about how many other networking events he had attended that week. So I asked him, "How do you find the time to follow up with all the people you meet?" He said, "I gave them my card. They'll call me when they need me." I said, "Think about an event you attended a month ago. Who did you meet and how would you get in touch with them? I'm going to get a Mountain Dew so you can have some time to think." He looked at me and said, "I'm sure I could find those cards somewhere if I looked hard enough." I smiled and said, "Will you?" I always say, "If you don't follow up, you were never there." You can steal that quote if you like. Take the time to reach out to people, meet them for coffee, and always connect with them on social media. You never know who may be your next best client or referral source.

TWO THINGS NOT TO DO AFTER A BUSINESS NETWORKING EVENT

Many networking groups send out a list of all of the attendees after their events. Many of my friends spam everyone on the list with their sales pitch. I've asked a few friends what they write in these emails. Do they say, "Hey, you were at the event and I was at the event, so we should meet for coffee so I can sell you my services."? Or "Hey, it was great seeing you at the event last night. I'd love to meet up for coffee so I can sell you my products."? How do they know the list is accurate? Some people on the list might not have even been there, and I doubt my friends talked to everyone on the list. Don't say it was great to catch up with you last night if you didn't really interact. Think about it. If 40 people go to a networking event and they all send an email to everyone who attended, every attendee will receive 39 unsolicited emails. Have you ever met someone at a networking event and known right away that you wouldn't do business with him? Well the group just gave him your name and email address.

The second thing not to do is what I call the bait and switch. This actually happened to me. A potential client said he wanted to meet because he was interested in joining my networking group. When I arrived for the meeting, he had his laptop open to show me his presentation. When we first met, I told him I wasn't interested in his business. Politely, I still spent 30 minutes watching his presentation. When it was over, I said, "As I told you when we met, I'm not interested in becoming a member of your team. When we spoke, you said you were interested in joining the group." He looked me in the eye and said, "No, I lied to get you to come today."

Okay, where do we start with how wrong this is? Of course, I can never recommend him to anyone, because he's dishonest, with a blatant disregard for the value of people's time, and he violates so many of the tips previously noted in this book! Please don't use the bait and switch move. It never ends well.

Kevin Willett

HOW TO STAY IN TOUCH WITH YOUR NETWORKING CONNECTIONS

People ask me all the time how I stay in touch with all my networking connections. I have to admit, as my network continues to grow, this does become very challenging. Here are a few things I do to stay in touch. I always thank people when they endorse me on LinkedIn. I'll talk a little bit more about that in another tip. Also on LinkedIn, I endorse people when I can, congratulate them when they get a new job, and wish them a happy birthday. When someone is celebrating a birthday or has a new job, I offer to meet up for coffee or have lunch to celebrate. This is a simple way to stay in touch with your networking contacts.

BUSINESS CARDS

DO YOUR BUSINESS CARDS LOOK GOOD?

Has anyone ever given you a business card that looked like it went through the laundry or maybe it had a coffee stain on it? What image did you get of that person? It probably wasn't a favorable one. The message they're sending is that they're sloppy and don't pay attention to details. There are so many affordable options for purchasing business cards, but if you must make your own at home, buy good card stock and make sure they're evenly cut with no frayed edges. Your business cards are part of your brand. Whether they're inexpensive or gold plated, take pride in their appearance.

DOES YOUR BUSINESS CARD SAY WHAT YOU DO?

The first cards I made for my computer consulting business, KMW Consulting, were really awesome looking, except for one major detail: They didn't say what I consulted on. So that goes into the epic fail category. Don't make people guess what you do. Chances are they won't bother to try, and your card will end up in the trash. Your card should also include your complete contact information. I received a card recently that had a phone number but no email address. Remember to include both, and use a font size and style that's easy to read. Putting your website address on your card is also a good idea. That gives people a chance to further review your business and get answers to questions they may not have asked when you met.

IT'S OKAY TO GIVE TWO CARDS

I was at a networking event and I met a guy who I had two referrals for, so I asked him for two business cards. Both people had asked me to find someone with his skills for specific jobs they needed done. The guy looked at me and said, "I only brought a few cards along, so I can only give you one. I need to save them for other people." I thought he was joking with me at first. When I realized he wasn't, I handed him the card back and said, "Never mind. I'll find someone else to do it." Don't leave home without enough cards. But be careful about going too far. People have given me 50 cards and asked me to pass them out, because they know I meet a lot of people. It's a bit bold to ask me or anyone else to pass out cards if you're not a client. So please understand, the majority of those cards will end up in the recycle bin.

LOOK AT THE BUSINESS CARD
BEFORE YOU PUT IT IN YOUR POCKET

Here's a cool idea I learned a while ago: When someone hands you a business card, take a moment to look at it and make a comment about it. I find most people put a lot of thought into their logo, or the colors they choose, or even the font, so they'll appreciate your comment. Have you ever passed your card to someone and he just slid it into his pocket? How did it make you feel? It makes me feel like I'll never hear from him again. Now if he spent just 30 seconds looking at the card and commenting, I would feel like he actually did enjoy talking with me and that I may hear from him again.

WRITE NOTES ON THE BACK OF BUSINESS CARDS

I have a friend who does an awesome job with this idea. Every time he attends a networking event, he makes notes about the people he meets on the back of their cards. He reviews the cards before he attends the next event for that group. It's really powerful when he can walk up to you and say, "Hey, last time we spoke you were writing a book. How's it coming along?" This makes the people he talks to feel great about themselves, because this guy hasn't seen them in a few months, but he still remembers what they spoke about.

Kevin Willett

SOCIAL MEDIA

ARE YOU MAKING IT EASY FOR PEOPLE TO CONNECT WITH YOU?

Have you ever tried to connect with someone on LinkedIn and found there were 10 people with the same name and most of them didn't have a profile picture on their account? What did you do? Most people simply give up and don't take the time to check out every profile trying to find someone. If you haven't completely filled out your profile, you may be missing out on connections. Also include a tasteful, if not professional, headshot of yourself to help people find you. A picture of your cat is not going to help me. If you're not using LinkedIn, sign up today. As a business professional, you must have an account on LinkedIn. Another thing, how many Facebook pages do you have? Email addresses? Less is best in this case. I want to use the one that will reach you.

GO OUTSIDE OF YOUR NETWORK

I met with a woman recently who had lost her job. When I suggested that she reach out to her LinkedIn connections for help, she told me all of her connections on LinkedIn worked for her former employer. She had never thought about connecting with vendors or customers or people outside her industry. She thought she would work at this company forever.

I have to admit, when I first started Friends of Kevin, I tried to connect with people who fit the profile of a potential client, never realizing that four years later I would decide to start the New England B2B Networking Group. I really wish I'd made a better effort to connect with those people who didn't fit the Friends of Kevin profile, because they're perfect for the New England B2B Networking Group.

So the next time you're tempted to dismiss someone who doesn't need your services, remember, they may have friends who do. I'm still surprised when my social media connections, people I've never met, send me clients. If I had refused their connection requests, I would never have had those clients.

WHY YOU SHOULD BE ACTIVE ON LINKEDIN

I'm constantly amazed by how many networkers aren't active on LinkedIn. I see people spending a lot of money to join various networking groups, but never taking the time to connect with their fellow group members on LinkedIn. For me, LinkedIn is essential to my success. Whenever I'm considering hosting an event in a new area, I use LinkedIn to reach out to people in the networking groups in that area, to see if they'd like to attend. I'm stunned at how many of these people aren't on LinkedIn, or if they are, they haven't bothered to connect with the other group members.

My friends, if you fail to do this, you're missing out on an incredible opportunity. By connecting with the people you know, you have a chance to see their connections and to link up with these new people as well. Now, I'm not saying just log on and connect with everyone your friends are connected to. If you see someone on LinkedIn who may be able to help you grow your business or vice versa, ask your common friend for an introduction through messaging. It's quick and simple. So this week, take the time to work on your LinkedIn profile and connect with your friends and business associates to help you expand your network.

PERSONALIZE YOUR LINKEDIN INVITATIONS

How do you feel when you get the standard LinkedIn invitation from a new connection? Does it make you feel special? Please never use the standard or the default setting, especially when you don't know the person.

Last week I received an invitation from someone who took the time to say he had heard great things about my group and looked forward to coming to an event to find out what all the buzz was about. I can assure you, I accepted his connection immediately and sent him a nice email asking how I could help him.

When I receive a default message on LinkedIn, my first thought is that this person is just trying to collect contacts or that my name showed up under people you may know. My friends, there's no excuse for not taking a few moments to customize your invitation. Not doing so is disrespectful to the person you're trying to connect with.

WHY YOU SHOULD THANK PEOPLE FOR ENDORSING YOU ON LINKEDIN

Most people never take the time to say thank you when someone endorses them on LinkedIn. This simple gesture will make you stand out from the crowd. A guy I don't know all that well endorsed me. I sent him a message thanking him and he responded with a really great message thanking me for all that I do and wishing me further success. I was having a really crappy day, but his simple response turned around my whole day. It's often the simple things in life, my friends, that will make you happy.

RECOMMENDATIONS AND ENDORSEMENTS

Let's make this tip really easy. Never write a recommendation for someone you haven't done business with. You're defeating the purpose of the recommendation if you're just writing it hoping the person will write one for you too. And don't ever, under any circumstances, request a recommendation from someone you don't know or haven't done business with.

Every week, a few people ask me to recommend them, although we've never done business together and I don't know them personally. What am I supposed to say about them? That they had the courage to ask a perfect stranger to write them a recommendation? Surely they've done business with people who can recommend them. Why aren't they asking them?

The same rules apply to endorsements. Don't randomly endorse people hoping they'll endorse you back. I see a lot of people leave comments on LinkedIn, wondering why people are endorsing them for things they don't even do. Don't be that person trying to collect as many endorsements as possible by endorsing everyone.

Personally, I don't value endorsements or recommendations, because I believe the majority of them are done for the wrong reasons. But that's just my opinion.

WHEN WAS THE LAST TIME YOU GOOGLED YOURSELF?

I'm surprised when I hear that people don't Google themselves. You want to monitor what's being said about you and your company. When you Google a friend of mine, the first thing that comes up is a picture of him in a diaper from a college party. Is that the image you want people to have of you? It's funny when you're still in school, but not when you're 30. So take a few minutes to Google yourself, to protect your brand. You may be surprised by what you see.

DON'T RANT ON SOCIAL MEDIA

So business isn't going well for you. I know a way to make it better, go on social media and tell people they're stupid because they don't do business with you. Sadly, I see this a lot on Facebook. My friends, telling me I'm stupid won't make me want to do business with you. If you need to vent, find a friend you can complain to when things aren't going well. Please never rant on social media. It makes you look unprofessional.

I HAVE A RIGHT TO MY OPINIONS

Whenever I'm out speaking about networking, I tell people to be careful about what they post on social media, because it can really hurt their image. One person in the group will always yell out, "I have a right to my opinion." I always smile and say, "Yes you do, and I have the right to be offended by it and not do business with you." For some reason, the room gets quiet after that. Most companies will Google people before they hire them or do business with them. Are your opinions costing you business?

DON'T MAKE THESE MISTAKES WHEN USING MEETUP

I really like Meetup.com, but I find many people don't make the most of it. How many profiles do you see with no picture, just a first name, and no details about what the person does? Why would you expect anyone to reach out to you when they don't know what you do or why you're on Meetup? I realize not everyone uses Meetup for business networking, and that's cool, but if you joined to connect with other rock climbers, put that in your profile. So stop reading for a minute, go grab yourself a Mountain Dew, and update your profile. If you're using Meetup to network, please join my groups at www.meetup.com/friendsofkevin and www.meetup.com/newenglandb2bnetworking.com

DON'T MAKE THESE MISTAKES WHEN USING LINKEDIN

I find that many people make mistakes on LinkedIn similar to those on Meetup. I still see lots of profiles with no profile picture or a picture of the person's cat. Many people don't bother to fill in the details about their business and what they do, so their description just says CEO of Company A. If you don't describe what your business does, why would you expect anyone to connect with you or consider doing business with you? My friends, never assume that everyone knows about your company. Take the time to describe what your company does and who it serves. If you do this, your success on LinkedIn will greatly improve. Stop reading this book right now, update your LinkedIn profile, and of course, be sure to connect with me there.

WHY DON'T THEY LIKE ME?

Have you ever tried to connect with someone on social media and they rejected you? Don't take it personally. Many of my friends will only connect with people they know personally or have done business with. Everyone has their own rules about who they'll network with. Most people are not like me. I connect with everyone I meet or with friends of friends who I haven't met (feel free to connect with me if you like). So please don't let your feelings get hurt if your "friend request" is rejected. It's not that they don't like you; it's just that they haven't read this book yet.

USE A CURRENT PICTURE

I really like my high school graduation picture, but sadly, I'm not that thin anymore and my hair is turning gray daily. I see so many people use pictures on social media or on their business cards that don't look anything like what they look like today. My friends, that's just silly. Resist any temptation you might have to do this. You might meet your contacts in real life one day. What will they think of you? I've walked around the coffee shop many times looking for people, saying to myself, "If that person were 20 years younger, they'd look exactly like the person I'm meeting," and then have them wave to me, saying, "Hi Kevin." My friends, we can't hold on to our youth, so use an up-to-date photo for networking.

SOCIAL MEDIA WILL NEVER REPLACE IN-PERSON NETWORKING

Nobody loves social media more than I do. I've made many incredible connections online that I might never have made otherwise. But social media is simply the beginning of the relationship. It flourishes once you meet your contacts in person. You can't read body language or hear passion about someone's business online. I find so many people want to sit at home and collect contacts online, and that's fine, but there's no better combination than in-person and online networking to really strengthen a relationship.

AFTERWORD

Thanks for taking the time to read my book. I do appreciate it. My only hope is that you learned at least one thing that can help you feel more comfortable at your next networking event.

As I reflect on the experience of writing this book, and hosting hundreds of networking events, the best advice I can leave you with is to step outside your comfort zone and sign up for a networking event today.

The book offers some great tips on networking, but I've found that everyone develops their own style and networking personality. Don't worry about trying to use every tip in the book. Hand pick the ones you like the best and try them at your next networking event. I promise you that each event will become a little easier and soon you will be a networking expert.

If you have any questions about networking or anything in the book, feel free to email me at Kevin@friendsofkevin.com or you can always call me. My number isn't too hard to find.

I would like to ask you for one favor. When you feel you don't need this book anymore, please don't put it on your bookshelf. Please write your name on the inside cover, bring it to your next networking event, and pass it on to someone who is new to networking so that we can both help them.

Thanks for being my Friend,

Kevin

Made in the USA
Middletown, DE
18 May 2015